Feminine Gospels

Also by Carol Ann Duffy

Standing Female Nude (1985)

Selling Manhattan (1987)

The Other Country (1990)

Mean Time (1993)

Penguin Selected Poems (1994)

The World's Wife (1999)

FOR CHILDREN

Meeting Midnight (1999)

Rumpelstiltskin and Other Grimm Tales (1999)

The Oldest Girl in the World (2000)

Underwater Farmyard (2002)

Queen Munch and Queen Nibble (2002)

AS EDITOR

I Wouldn't Thank You for a Valentine (1992)

Stopping for Death (1996)

Anvil New Poets (1996)

Time's Tidings (1999)

Hand in Hand (2001)

CAROL ANN DUFFY

Feminine Gospels

PICADOR

First published 2002 by Picador
an imprint of Pan Macmillan Ltd
Pan Macmillan, 20 New Wharf Road, London N1 9RR
Basingstoke and Oxford
Associated companies throughout the world
www.panmacmillan.com

ISBN 0 330 48643 8

1 3 5 7 9 8 6 4 2

A CIP catalogue record for this book is available from
the British Library.

Typeset by SX Composing DTP, Rayleigh, Essex
Printed and bound in Great Britain by
Mackays of Chatham plc, Chatham, Kent

NESTA – the National Endowment for Science, Technology and the Arts – was
set up in 1998 to support innovation and creative potential in the UK

for my brothers –

Frank, Adrian, Eugene and Tim

Contents

Acknowledgements

Poetry Review; *The Rialto*;
The Times Literary Supplement; Waterstones;
The Year of the Artist / Wolverhampton City Council;
BBC Radio.

Carol Ann Duffy gratefully acknowledges a NESTA Fellowship.

The Long Queen

The Long Queen couldn't die.
Young when she bowed her head
for the cold weight of the crown, she'd looked
at the second son of the earl, the foreign prince,
the heir to the duke, the lord, the baronet, the count,
then taken Time for a husband. Long live the Queen.

What was she queen of? Women, girls,
spinsters and hags, matrons, wet nurses,
witches, widows, wives, mothers of all these.
Her word of law was in their bones, in the graft
of their hands, in the wild kicks of their dancing.
No girl born who wasn't the Long Queen's always child.

Unseen, she ruled and reigned; some said
in a castle, some said in a tower in the dark heart
of a wood, some said out and about in rags, disguised,
sorting the bad from the good. She sent her explorers away
in their creaking ships and was queen of more, of all the dead
when they lived if they did so female. All hail to the Queen.

What were her laws? *Childhood*: whether a girl
awoke from the bad dream of the worst, or another
swooned into memory, bereaved, bereft, or a third one
wrote it all down like a charge-sheet, or the fourth never left,
scouring the markets and shops for her old books and toys –
no girl growing who wasn't the apple of the Long Queen's eye.

Blood: proof, in the Long Queen's colour,
royal red, of intent; the pain when a girl
first bled to be insignificant, no cause for complaint,

and this is to be monthly, linked to the moon, till middle age
when the law would change. *Tears*: salt pearls, bright jewels
for the Long Queen's fingers to weigh as she counted their sorrow.

Childbirth: most to lie on the birthing beds,
push till the room screamed scarlet and children
bawled and slithered into their arms, sore flowers;
some to be godmother, aunt, teacher, teller of tall tales,
but all who were there to swear that the pain was worth it.
No mother bore daughter not named to honour the Queen.

And her pleasures were stories, true or false,
that came in the evening, drifting up on the air
to the high window she watched from, confession
or gossip, scandal or anecdote, secrets, her ear tuned
to the light music of girls, the drums of women, the faint strings
of the old. Long Queen. All her possessions for a moment of time.

The Map-Woman

A woman's skin was a map of the town
where she'd grown from a child.
When she went out, she covered it up
with a dress, with a shawl, with a hat,
with mitts or a muff, with leggings, trousers
or jeans, with an ankle-length cloak, hooded
and fingertip-sleeved. But – birthmark, tattoo –
the A-Z street-map grew, a precise second skin,
broad if she binged, thin when she slimmed,
a precis of where to end or go back or begin.

Over her breast was the heart of the town,
from the Market Square to the Picture House
by way of St Mary's Church, a triangle
of alleys and streets and walks, her veins
like shadows below the lines of the map, the river
an artery snaking north to her neck. She knew
if you crossed the bridge at her nipple, took a left
and a right, you would come to the graves,
the grey-haired teachers of English and History,
the soldier boys, the Mayors and Councillors,

the beloved mothers and wives, the nuns and priests,
their bodies fading into the earth like old print
on a page. You could sit on a wooden bench
as a wedding pair ran, ringed, from the church,
confetti skittering over the marble stones,
the big bell hammering hail from the sky, and wonder
who you would marry and how and where and when
you would die; or find yourself in the coffee house

nearby, waiting for time to start, your tiny face
trapped in the window's bottle-thick glass like a fly.

And who might you see, short-cutting through
the Grove to the Square – that line there, the edge
of a fingernail pressed on her flesh – in the rain,
leaving your empty cup, to hurry on after
calling their name? When she showered, the map
gleamed on her skin, blue-black ink from a nib.
She knew you could scoot down Greengate Street,
huddling close to the High House, the sensible shops,
the Swan Hotel, till you came to the Picture House,
sat in the musty dark watching the Beatles

run for a train or Dustin Hoffman screaming
Elaine! Elaine! Elaine! or the spacemen in 2001
floating to Strauss. She sponged, soaped, scrubbed;
the prison and hospital stamped on her back,
the park neat on her belly, her navel marking the spot
where the empty bandstand stood, the river again,
heading south, clear as an operation scar,
the war memorial facing the railway station
where trains sighed on the platforms, pining
for Glasgow, London, Liverpool. She knew

you could stand on the railway bridge, waving
goodbye to strangers who stared as you vanished
into the belching steam, tasting future time
on the tip of your tongue. She knew you could run
the back way home – there it was on her thigh –
taking the southern road then cutting off to the left,
the big houses anchored behind their calm green lawns,
the jewels of conkers falling down at your feet,

then duck and dive down Nelson and Churchill
and Kipling and Milton Way until you were home.

She didn't live there now. She lived down south,
abroad, en route, up north, on a plane or train
or boat, on the road, in hotels, in the back of cabs,
on the phone; but the map was under her stockings,
under her gloves, under the soft silk scarf at her throat,
under her chiffon veil, a delicate braille. Her left knee
marked the grid of her own estate. When she knelt
she felt her father's house pressing into the bone,
heard in her head the looped soundtrack of then –
a tennis ball repeatedly thumping a wall,

an ice-cream van crying and hurrying on, a snarl
of children's shrieks from the overgrown land
where the houses ran out. The motorway groaned
just out of sight. She knew you could hitch
from Junction 13 and knew of a girl who had not
been seen since she did; had heard of a kid who'd run
across all six lanes for a dare before he was tossed
by a lorry into the air like a doll. But the motorway
was flowing away, was a roaring river of metal
and light, cheerio, au revoir, auf wiedersehen, ciao.

She stared in the mirror as she got dressed,
both arms raised over her head, the roads
for east and west running from shoulder
to wrist, the fuzz of woodland or countryside under
each arm. Only her face was clear, her fingers
smoothing in cream, her baby-blue eyes unsure
as they looked at themselves. But her body was certain,
an inch to the mile, knew every nook and cranny,

cul-de-sac, stile, back road, high road, low road,
one-way street of her past. There it all was, back

to front in the glass. She piled on linen, satin, silk,
leather, wool, perfume and mousse and went out.
She got in a limousine. The map perspired
under her clothes. She took a plane. The map seethed
on her flesh. She spoke in a foreign tongue.
The map translated everything back to herself.
She turned out the light and a lover's hands
caressed the map in the dark from north to south,
lost tourists wandering here and there, all fingers
and thumbs, as their map flapped in the breeze.

So one day, wondering where to go next,
she went back, drove a car for a night and a day,
till the town appeared on her left, the stale cake
of the castle crumbled up on the hill; and she hired
a room with a view and soaked in the bath.
When it grew dark, she went out, thinking
she knew the place like the back of her hand,
but something was wrong. She got lost in arcades,
in streets with new names, in precincts
and walkways, and found that what was familiar

was only facade. Back in her hotel room, she stripped
and lay on the bed. As she slept, her skin sloughed
like a snake's, the skin of her legs like stockings, silvery,
sheer, like the long gloves of the skin of her arms,
the papery camisole from her chest a perfect match
for the tissuey socks of the skin of her feet. Her sleep
peeled her, lifted a honeymoon thong from her groin,
a delicate bra of skin from her breasts, and all of it

patterned A to Z; a small cross where her parents' skulls
grinned at the dark. Her new skin showed barely a mark.

She woke and spread out the map on the floor. What
was she looking for? Her skin was her own small ghost,
a shroud to be dead in, a newspaper for old news
to be read in, gift-wrapping, litter, a suicide letter.
She left it there, dressed, checked out, got in the car.
As she drove, the town in the morning sun glittered
behind her. She ate up the miles. Her skin itched,
like a rash, like a slow burn, felt stretched, as though
it belonged to somebody else. Deep in the bone
old streets tunnelled and burrowed, hunting for home.

Beautiful

She was born from an egg,
a daughter of the gods,
divinely fair, a pearl, drop-dead
gorgeous, beautiful, a peach,
a child of grace, a stunner, in her face
the starlike sorrows of immortal eyes.
Who looked there, loved.

She won the heart
of every man she saw.
They stood in line, sighed,
knelt, beseeched *Be Mine*.
She married one,
but every other mother's son
swore to be true to her
till death, enchanted
by the perfume of her breath,
her skin's celebrity.

So when she took a lover, fled,
was nowhere to be seen,
her side of the bed unslept in, cold,
the small coin of her wedding ring
left on the bedside table like a tip,
the wardrobe empty
of the drama of her clothes,
it was War.

A thousand ships –
on every one a thousand men,
each heaving at an oar,

each with her face
before his stinging eyes,
her name tattooed
upon the muscle of his arm,
a handkerchief she'd dropped once
for his lucky charm,
each seeing her as a local girl
made good, the girl next door,
a princess with the common touch,
queen of his heart, pin-up, superstar,
the heads of every coin he'd tossed,
the smile on every note he'd bet at cards –
bragged and shoved across a thousand miles of sea.

Meanwhile, lovely she lay high up
in a foreign castle's walls, clasped
in a hero's brawn, loved and loved
and loved again, her cries
like the bird of calamity's,
drifting down to the boys at the gates
who marched now to the syllables of her name.

Beauty is fame. Some said
she turned into a cloud
and floated home,
falling there like rain, or tears,
upon her husband's face.
Some said her lover woke
to find her gone,
his sword and clothes gone too,
before they sliced a last grin in his throat.

Some swore they saw her smuggled
on a boat dressed as a boy,

rowed to a ship which slid away at dusk,
beckoned by the finger of the moon.
Some vowed that they were in the crowd
that saw her hung, stared up at her body
as it swung there on the creaking rope,
and noticed how the black silk of her dress
clung to her form, a stylish shroud.

Her maid, who loved her most,
refused to say one word
to anyone at any time or place,
would not describe
one aspect of her face
or tell one anecdote about her life and loves.

But lived alone
and kept a little bird inside a cage.

*   *   *

She never aged.
She sashayed up the river
in a golden barge,
her fit girls giggling at her jokes.
She'd tumbled from a rug at Caesar's feet,
seen him kneel to pick her up
and felt him want her as he did.
She had him gibbering in bed by twelve.

But now, she rolled her carpet on the sand,
put up her crimson tent, laid out
silver plate with grapes and honey, yoghurt,
roasted songbirds, gleaming figs, soft wines,
and soaked herself in jasmine-scented milk.

She knew her man. She knew that when
he stood that night, ten times her strength,
inside the fragrant boudoir of her tent,
and saw her wrapped in satins like a gift,
his time would slow to nothing, zilch,
until his tongue could utter in her mouth.
She reached and pulled him down
to Alexandria, the warm muddy Nile.

Tough beauty. She played with him
at dice, rolled sixes in the dust,
cleaned up, slipped her gambling hand
into his pouch and took his gold, bit it,
Caesar's head between her teeth.
He crouched with lust. On her couch,
she lay above him, painted him,
her lipstick smeared on his mouth,
her powder blushing on his stubble,
the turquoise of her eyes over his lids.
She matched him glass for glass
in drinking games: sucked lemons, licked
at salt, swallowed something from a bottle
where a dead rat floated, gargled doubles
over trebles, downed a liquid fire in one,
lit a coffee bean in something else, blew it,
gulped, tipped chasers down her throat,
pints down her neck, and held her drink
until the big man slid beneath the table, wrecked.

She watched him hunt. He killed a stag.
She hacked the heart out, held it,
dripping, in the apron of her dress.
She watched him exercise in arms.
His soldiers marched, eyes right, her way.

She let her shawl slip down to show
her shoulders, breasts, and every man
that night saw them again and prayed
her name. She waved him off to war,
then pulled on boy's clothes, crept
at dusk into his camp, his shadowed tent,
touched him, made him fuck her as a lad.
He had no choice, upped sticks,
downed tools, went back with her,
swooned on her flesh for months,
her fingers in his ears, her kiss
closing his eyes, her stories blethering
on his lips: of armies changing sides,
of cities lost forever in the sea, of snakes.

   *   *   *

The camera loved her, close-up, back-lit,
adored the waxy pouting of her mouth,
her sleepy, startled gaze. She breathed
the script out in her little voice. They filmed her
famous, filmed her beautiful. Guys fell
in love, dames copied her. An athlete
licked the raindrops from her fingertips
to quench his thirst. She married him.
The US whooped.

They filmed her harder, harder, till her hair
was platinum, her teeth gems, her eyes
sapphires pressed by a banker's thumb.
She sang to camera one, gushed
at the greased-up lens, her skin investors' gold,
her fingernails mother-of-pearl, her voice
champagne to sip from her lips. A poet came,

found her wondrous to behold. She married him.
The whole world swooned.

Dumb beauty. She slept in an eye-mask, naked,
drugged, till the maid came, sponged
at her puffy face, painted the beauty on in beige,
pinks, blues. Then it was coffee, pills, booze,
Frank on the record-player, it was put on the mink,
get in the studio car. Somebody big was watching her –
white fur, mouth at the mike, under the lights. *Happy
Birthday to you. Happy Birthday, Mr President.*
The audience drooled.

They filmed on, deep, dumped what they couldn't use
on the cutting-room floor, filmed more, quiet please,
action, cut, quiet please, action, cut, quiet please,
action, cut, till she couldn't die when she died,
couldn't get older, ill, couldn't stop saying the lines
or singing the tunes. The smoking cop who watched
as they zipped her into the body-bag noticed
her strong resemblance to herself, the dark roots
of her pubic hair.

*   *   *

Dead, she's elegant bone
in mud, ankles crossed,
knees clamped, hands clasped,
empty head. You know her name.

Plain women turned in the streets
where her shadow fell, under
her spell, swore that what she wore
they'd wear, coloured their hair.

The whole town came
to wave at her on her balcony,
to stare and stare and stare.
Her face was surely a star.

Beauty is fate. They gaped
as her bones danced
in a golden dress in the arms
of her wooden prince, gawped

as she posed alone
in front of the Taj Mahal,
betrayed, beautifully pale.
The cameras gibbered away.

Act like a fucking princess –
how they loved her,
the men from the press –
Give us a smile, cunt.

And her blue eyes widened
to take it all in: the flashbulbs,
the half-mast flags, the acres of flowers,
History's stinking breath in her face.

The Diet

The diet worked like a dream. No sugar,
salt, dairy, fat, protein, starch or alcohol.
By the end of week one, she was half a stone
shy of ten and shrinking, skipping breakfast,
lunch, dinner, thinner; a fortnight in, she was
eight stone; by the end of the month, she was skin
and bone.

        She starved on, stayed in, stared in
the mirror, svelter, slimmer. The last apple
aged in the fruit bowl, untouched. The skimmed milk
soured in the fridge, unsupped. Her skeleton preened
under its tight flesh dress. She was all eyes,
all cheekbones, had guns for hips. Not a stitch
in the wardrobe fitted.

           What passed her lips? Air,
water. She was Anorexia's true daughter, a slip
of a girl, a shadow, dwindling away. One day,
the width of a stick, she started to grow smaller –
child-sized, doll-sized, the height of a thimble.
She sat at her open window and the wind
blew her away.

        Seed small, she was out and about,
looking for home. An empty beer bottle rolled
in the gutter. She crawled in, got drunk on the dregs,
started to sing, down, out, nobody's love. Tiny others
joined in. They raved all night. She woke alone,
head splitting, mouth dry, hungry and cold, and made
for the light.

She found she could fly on the wind,
could breathe, if it rained, underwater. That night,
she went to a hotel bar that she knew and floated into
the barman's eye. She slept for hours, left at dawn
in a blink, in a wink, drifted away on a breeze.
Minute, she could suit herself from here on in, go
where she pleased.

She stayed near people,
lay in the tent of a nostril like a germ, dwelled
in the caves of an ear. She lived in a tear, swam
clear, moved south to a mouth, kipped in the chap
of a lip. She loved flesh and blood, wallowed
in mud under fingernails, dossed in a fold of fat
on a waist.

But when she squatted the tip of a tongue,
she was gulped, swallowed, sent down the hatch
in a river of wine, bottoms up, cheers, fetched up
in a stomach just before lunch. She crouched
in the lining, hearing the avalanche munch of food,
then it was carrots, peas, courgettes, potatoes,
gravy and meat.

Then it was sweet. Then it was stilton,
roquefort, weisslacker-käse, gex; it was smoked salmon
with scrambled eggs, hot boiled ham, plum flan, frogs'
legs. She knew where she was all right, clambered
onto the greasy breast of a goose, opened wide, then
chomped and chewed and gorged; inside the Fat Woman now,
trying to get out.

The Woman Who Shopped

went out with a silver shilling, willing to buy, bought
an apple, red as first love's heart, bright as her eye,
had plenty of change, purchased a hat with a brim,
walked with a suitor under its shadow, ditched him;

saved up a pound, a fiver, a tenner, haggled the price
of a dancing dress down to a snip, spent the remainder
on shoes, danced from the house down the street, tapped
to the centre of town where the sales had commenced,

applied for a job for the wage and the bonus, blew it
on clothes; wanted a wedding, a wedding dress, groom,
married him, wanted a honeymoon, went on one,
looked at the gold of her ring as it flashed in the sun;

flew away home to furnish each room of the house,
shuffle his plastic with hers, deal them out in the shops
for cutlery, crockery, dishwashers, bed linen, TV sets,
three-piece suites, stereos, microwaves, telephones,

curtains and mirrors and rugs; shrugged at the cost,
then fixed up a loan, filled up the spare room with boxes
of merchandise, unopened cartons, over-stuffed bags;
went on the Internet, shopped in America, all over Europe,

tapping her credit card numbers all night, ordering
swimming pools, caravans, saunas; when they arrived,
stacked up on the lawn, she fled, took to the streets,
where the lights from the shops ran like paint in the rain,

and pressed her face to the pane of the biggest and best;
the happy shoppers were fingering silk, holding cashmere
close to their cheeks, dancing with fur; she slept there,
curled in the doorway, six shopping bags at her feet.

*   *   *

Stone cold when she woke, she was stone, was concrete
and glass, her eyes windows squinting back at the light,
her brow a domed roof, her thoughts neon, flashing on
and off, vague in the daylight. She seemed to be kneeling

or squatting, her shoulders broad and hunched, her hands
huge and part of the pavement. She looked down. Her skirts
were glass doors opening and closing, her stockings were
moving stairs, her shoes were lifts, going up, going down:

first floor for perfumery and cosmetics, ladies' accessories,
lingerie, fine jewels and watches; second for homewares,
furniture, travel goods, luggage; third floor for menswear,
shaving gear, shoes; fourth floor for books, toyland,

childrenswear, sports; fifth floor for home entertainment,
pianos, musical instruments, beauty and hair. Her ribs
were carpeted red, her lungs glittered with chandeliers
over the singing tills, her gut was the food hall, hung

with fat pink hams, crammed with cheeses, fruits, wines,
truffles and caviar. She loved her own smell, sweat and Chanel,
loved the crowds jostling and thronging her bones, loved
the credit cards swiping themselves in her blood, her breath

was gift wrapping, the whisper of tissue and string, she loved
the changing rooms of her heart, the rooftop restaurant
in her eyes, the dark basement under the lower ground floor
where juggernauts growled, unloading their heavy crates.

The sky was unwrapping itself, ripping itself into shreds.
She would have a sale and crowds would queue overnight
at her cunt, desperate for bargains. Light blazed from her now.
Birds shrieked and voided themselves in her stone hair.

Work

To feed one, she worked from home,
took in washing, ironing, sewing.
One small mouth, a soup-filled spoon,
life was a dream.

To feed two,
she worked outside, sewed seeds, watered,
threshed, scythed, gathered barley, wheat, corn.
Twins were born. To feed four,

she grafted harder, second job in the alehouse,
food in the larder, food on the table,
she was game, able. Feeding ten
was a different kettle,

was factory gates
at first light, oil, metal, noise, machines.
To feed fifty, she toiled, sweated, went
on the night shift, schlepped, lifted.

For a thousand more, she built streets,
for double that, high-rise flats. Cities grew,
her brood doubled, peopled skyscrapers,
trebled. To feed more, more,

she dug underground, tunnelled,
laid down track, drove trains. Quadruple came,
multiplied, she built planes, outflew sound.
Mother to millions now,

she flogged TVs,
designed PCs, ripped CDs, burned DVDs.
There was no stopping her. She slogged
night and day at Internet shopping.

A billion named,
she trawled the seas, hoovered fish, felled trees,
grazed beef, sold cheap fast food, put in
a 90-hour week. Her offspring swelled. She fed

the world, wept rain, scattered the teeth in her head
for grain, swam her tongue in the river to spawn,
sickened, died, lay in a grave, worked, to the bone,
her fingers twenty-four seven.

Tall

Then, like a christening gift or a wish arriving
later in life, the woman had height, grew tall,
was taller daily.

Day one saw her rising at 8 foot
bigger than any man. She knelt in the shower
as if she were praying for rain. Her clothes
would be curtains and eiderdowns, towels and rugs.

Out. Eye-high with street lamps, she took a walk
downtown. Somebody whooped. She stooped,
hands on both knees,

and stared at his scared face,
the red heart tattooed on his small chest. He turned
and fled like a boy.

On. A tree dangled an apple
at bite-height. She bit it. A traffic-light stuttered
on red, went out. She lit it. Personal birds
sang on her ears. She whistled.

Further. Taller
as she went, she glanced into upper windows
in passing, saw lovers in the rented rooms
over shops, saw an old man long dead in a chair,
paused there, her breath on the glass.

She bowed herself into a bar, ordered a stiff drink.
It came on the rocks, on the house. A drunk
passed out or fainted. She pulled up a stool, sat
at the bar with her knees

                              under her chin, called
for another gin, a large one. She saw a face, high
in the mirror behind the top shelf. Herself.

Day two, she was hungover, all over, her head
in her hands in the hall, her feet at the top
of the stairs, more tall.

                    She needed a turret,
found one, day three, on the edge of town, moved in,
her head in the clouds now, showering in rain.

But pilgrims came –
small women with questions and worries, men
on stilts. She was 30 foot, growing, could see for miles.

So day six, she upped sticks, horizon-bound
in seven-league boots. Local crowds swarmed
round her feet, chanting.

                    She cured no one. Grew.
The moon came closer at night, its scarred face
an old mirror. She slept outdoors, stretched
across empty fields or sand.

　　　　　　The stars trembled. Taller
was colder, aloner, no wiser. What could she see
up there? She told them what kind of weather
was heading their way –

　　　　　　dust storms over the Pyramids,
hurricanes over the USA, floods in the UK –
but by now the people were tiny

　　　　　　and far away, and she
was taller than Jupiter, Saturn, the Milky Way. Nothing
to see. She looked back and howled.

　　　　　　She stooped low
and caught their souls in her hands as they fell
from the burning towers.

Loud

Parents with mutilated children have been turned away from the empty hospital and told to hire smugglers to take them across the border to Quetta, a Pakistani frontier city at least six hours away by car.

(Afghanistan, 28 October 2001)

The News had often made her shout,
but one day her voice ripped out of her throat
like a firework, with a terrible sulphurous crack
that made her jump, a flash of light in the dark.
Now she was loud.

Before, she'd been easily led,
one of the crowd, joined in with the national whoop
for the winning goal, the boos for the bent MP, the cheer
for the royal kiss on the balcony. Not any more. Now
she could roar.

She practised alone at home, found
she could call abroad without using the phone, could sing
like an orchestra in the bath, could yawn like thunder
watching TV. She switched to the News. It was all about
Muslims, Christians, Jews.

Then her scream was a huge bird
that flew her away into the dark; each vast wing a shriek,
awful to hear, the beak the sickening hiss of a thrown spear.
She stayed up there all night, in the wind and rain, wailing,
uttering lightning.

Down, she was pure sound, rumbling
like an avalanche. She bit radios, swallowed them, gargled
their News, till the words were – *ran into the church and sprayed
the congregation with bullets no one has claimed* – gibberish, crap,
in the cave of her mouth.

Her voice stomped through the city,
shouting the odds, shaking the bells awake in their towers.
She yelled through the countryside, swelling the rivers, felling
the woods. She put out to sea, screeching and bellowing,
spewing brine.

She bawled at the moon and it span away
into space. She hollered into the dark where fighter planes
buzzed at her face. She howled till every noise in the world
sang in the spit on the tip of her tongue: the shriek of a bomb,
the bang of a gun,

the prayers of the priest, the pad of the feet
in the mosque, the casual rip of the post, the mothers' sobs,
the thump of the drop, the President's cough, the screams
of the children cowering under their pews, loud, loud,
louder, the News.

History

She woke up old at last, alone,
bones in a bed, not a tooth
in her head, half dead, shuffled
and limped downstairs
in the rag of her nightdress,
smelling of pee.

Slurped tea, stared
at her hand – twigs, stained gloves –
wheezed and coughed, pulled on
the coat that hung from a hook
on the door, lay on the sofa,
dozed, snored.

She was History.
She'd seen them ease him down
from the Cross, his mother gasping
for breath, as though his death
was a difficult birth, the soldiers spitting,
spears in the earth;

been there
when the fishermen swore he was back
from the dead; seen the basilicas rise
in Jerusalem, Constantinople, Sicily; watched
for a hundred years as the air of Rome
turned into stone;

       witnessed the wars,
the bloody crusades, knew them by date
and by name, Bannockburn, Passchendaele,
Babi Yar, Vietnam. She'd heard the last words
of the martyrs burnt at the stake, the murderers
hung by the neck,

       seen up-close
how the saint whistled and spat in the flames,
how the dictator strutting on stuttering film
blew out his brains, how the children waved
their little hands from the trains. She woke again,
cold, in the dark,

      in the empty house.
Bricks through the window now, thieves
in the night. When they rang on her bell
there was nobody there; fresh graffiti sprayed
on her door, shit wrapped in a newspaper posted
onto the floor.

Sub

I came on in extra time in '66, my breasts
bandaged beneath my no. 13 shirt, and put it in
off the head, the back of the heel, the left foot
from 30 yards out, hat-trick. If they'd thought
the game was all over, it was now. I felt secure
as I danced in my dazzling whites with the Cup –
tampon – but skipped the team bath with the lads,
sipped my champagne in the solitary shower
as the blood and soap suds mingled to pink.
They sang my name on the other side of the steam.

Came on too in the final gasps of the Grand Slam clincher,
scooped up the ball from the back of the scrum, ran
like the wind, bandaged again, time of the month
likewise, wiggled, weaved, waved at the crowd, slipped
like soap through muddy hands, liked that, slid
between legs, nursing the precious egg of the ball,
then flung myself like breaking surf over the line
for the winning try, converted it, was carried
shoulder high by the boys as the whistle blew.
They roared my name through mouthfuls of broken teeth.

Ringo had flu when the Fab Four toured Down
Under. Minus a drummer, the gig was a bummer
till I stepped in, digits ringed, sticked, skinned,
in a Beatle skirt, mop-topped, fringed, to wink
at Paul, quip with John, climb on the drums,
clever fingered and thumbed, give it four to the bar,
give it *yeah yeah yeah*. The screams were lava,
hot as sex, and every seat in the house was wet.

We sang *Help!*, *Day Tripper*, *Money*, *This Boy*,
Girl, *She Loves You* – John, Paul, George and Moi.

It was one small step for a man for Neil
to stand on the Moon, a small hop for me
to stand in for Buzz, bounce in my moon-suit
over the dust, waving a flag. I knelt, scooped out
a hole in the powdery ground, and buried a box
with a bottle of malt, chocolates, Emily Dickinson's
poems. Ground Control barked down the line. *Houston,*
we don't have a problem, I said. It comforts me now,
the thought of them there, when I look at the moon.
Quietly there on the moon, the things that I like.

And when Beefy fell sick in the final Test,
I stepped up, two of his boxes over my chest,
and hooked a four from the first of Lillee's balls.
He bowled so fast you could hear his fingers click
as he spun off the seam. I lolled at the crease –
five months gone – and looped and hooped them about
like a dream, googlies, bosies, chinamen, zooters,
balls that dipped, flipped, nipped, whipped
at the wicket like bombs. I felt the first kick
of my child; whacked a century into the crowd.

Motherhood then kept me busy at home till my girl
started school. Not match-fit, I was talked
into management when Taylor went, caretaker role,
jacked that in after the World Cup win – Beckham
free-kick in extra time – and agreed on a whim to slim
to the weight of a boy, ride the winner at Aintree –
Bobbyjo, '99 – when the jockey dislocated his neck.
After that, I pulled right back, signed up to write

a book of my life and times, though I did play guitar
for the Band in LA when Bob gave me the call.

And when I look back – or my grandchildren ask me
what it was like to put Mohammed Ali on the deck
when Cooper was scratched from the scrap, or stand in
for Graham Hill to be Formula One Grand Champ
in the fastest recorded speed, or to dress up
as Borg in bandana and wig and steal the fifth set
at Wimbledon from under – *You cannot be serious* –
McEnroe's nose, or to kneel, best of all, first woman there,
on the Moon and gaze at the beautiful faraway earth –
what I think to myself is this:

The Virgin's Memo

maybe not abscesses, acne, asthma,
son, maybe not boils,
maybe not cancer
or diarrhoea
or tinnitus of the inner ear,
maybe not fungus,
maybe rethink the giraffe,
maybe not herpes, son,
or (text illegible)
or jellyfish
or (untranslatable)
maybe not leprosy or lice,
the menopause or mice, mucus, son,
neuralgia, nits,
maybe not body odour,
piles,
quicksand, quagmires,
maybe not rats, son, rabies, rattlesnakes,
shite,
and maybe hang fire on the tarantula,
the unicorn's lovely,
but maybe not veruccas
or wasps,
or (text illegible)
or (untranslatable)
maybe not . . .

Anon

If she were here
she'd forget who she was,
it's been so long,
maybe a nurse, a nanny,
maybe a nun –
Anon.

A girl I met
was willing to bet
that she still lived on –
Anon –
but had packed it all in,
the best verb, the right noun,
for a life in the sun.

A woman I knew
kept her skull
on a shelf in a room –
Anon's –
and swore that one day
as she worked at her desk
it cleared its throat
as though it had something
to get off its chest.

But I know best –
how she passed on her pen
like a baton
down through the years,
with a hey nonny
hey nonny
hey nonny no –
Anon.

The Laughter of Stafford Girls' High

(for T.W.)

It was a girl in the Third Form, Carolann Clare,
who, bored with the lesson, the rivers of England –
Brathay, Coquet, Crake, Dee, Don, Goyt,
Rothay, Tyne, Swale, Tees, Wear, Wharfe . . .
had passed a note, which has never been found,
to the classmate in front, Emily Jane, a girl
who adored the teacher, Miss V. Dunn MA,
steadily squeaking her chalk on the board –
Allen, Clough, Duddon, Feugh, Greta, Hindburn,
Irwell, Kent, Leven, Lowther, Lune, Sprint . . .
but who furtively opened the folded note,
torn from the back of the King James Bible, read
what was scribbled there and laughed out loud.

It was a miserable, lowering winter's day. The girls
had been kept indoors at break – Wet Play
in the Hall – the windows tall and thin,
sad with rain like a long list of watery names –
Rawthey, Roeburn, Skirfare, Troutbeck, Wash . . .
likewise, the sound of the laugh of Emily Jane
was a liquid one, a gurgle, a ripple, a dribble,
a babble, a gargle, a plash, a splash of a laugh
like the sudden jackpot leap of a silver fish
in the purse of a pool. No fool, Emily Jane
clamped her turquoisey hand – her fountain pen leaked –
to her mouth; but the laugh was out, was at large,
was heard by the pupil twinned to her double desk –

Rosemary Beth – the brace on whose jiggly teeth
couldn't restrain the gulping giggle she gave
which caused Miss Dunn to spin round. *Perhaps,*
she said, *We can all share the joke?* But Emily Jane
had scrunched and dropped the note with the joke
to the floor and kicked it across to Jennifer Kay
who snorted and toed it to Marjorie May
who spluttered and heeled it backwards
to Jessica Kate. *Girls!* By now, every girl in the form
had started to snigger or snicker or titter or chuckle
or chortle till the classroom came to the boil
with a brothy mirth. *Girls!* Miss Dunn's shrill voice
scraped Top G and only made matters worse.

Five minutes passed in a cauldron of noise.
No one could seem to stop. Each tried holding
her breath or thinking of death or pinching
her thigh, only to catch the eye of a pal,
a crimson, shaking, silent girl, and explode
through the nose in a cackling sneeze. *Thank you!*
Please! screeched Miss Dunn, clapping her hands
as though she applauded the choir they'd become,
a percussion of trills and whoops filling the room
like birds in a cage. But then came a triple rap
at the door and in stalked Miss Fife, Head of Maths,
whose cold equations of eyes scanned the desks
for a suitable scapegoat. *Stand up, Geraldine Ruth.*

Geraldine Ruth got to her feet, a pale girl, a girl
who looked, in the stale classroom light, like a sketch
for a girl, a first draft to be crumpled and crunched
and tossed away like a note. She cleared her throat,
raising her eyes, water and sky, to look at Miss Fife.

The girls who were there that day never forgot
how invisible crayons seemed to colour in
Geraldine Ruth, white face to puce, mousey hair
suddenly gifted with health and youth, and how –
as Miss Fife demanded what was the meaning of this –
her lips split from the closed bud of a kiss
to the daisy chain of a grin and how then she yodelled
a laugh with the full, open, blooming rose of her throat,

a flower of merriment. *What's the big joke?*
thundered Miss Fife as Miss Dunn began again
to clap, as gargling Geraldine Ruth collapsed
in a heap on her desk, as the rest of the class
hollered and hooted and howled. Miss Fife strode
on sharp heels to the blackboard, snatched up
a finger of chalk and jabbed and slashed out
a word. *SILENCE*. But the class next door,
Fourth Years learning the Beaufort scale with Miss Batt,
could hear the commotion. Miss Batt droned on –
Nought, calm; one, light air; two, light breeze; three,
gentle . . . four, moderate . . . five, fresh . . . six, strong breeze;
seven, moderate gale . . . Stephanie Fay started to laugh.

What's so amusing, Stephanie Fay? barked Miss Batt.
What's so amusing? echoed unwitting Miss Dunn
on the other side of the wall. *Precisely what's*
so amusing? chorused Miss Fife. The Fourth Years
shrieked with amazed delight and one wag,
Angela Joy, popped her head in the jaws of her desk
and bellowed *What's so amusing? What's so*
amusing? into its musty yawn. The Third Form
guffawed afresh at the sound of the Fourth
and the noise of the two combined was heard
by the First Form, trying to get Shakespeare by heart

to the beat of the ruler of Mrs Mackay. *Don't look
at your books, look at me. After three. Friends,*

Romans, Countrymen . . . What's so amusing? rapped out
Mrs Mackay as the First Years chirruped
and trilled like baby birds in a nest at a worm;
but she heard for herself, appalled, the chaos
coming in waves through the wall and clipped
to the door. Uproar. And her Head of Lower School!
It was then that Mrs Mackay made mistake number one,
leaving her form on its own while she went to see
to the forms of Miss Batt and Miss Dunn. The moment
she'd gone, the room blossomed with paper planes,
ink bombs, whistles, snatches of song, and the class clown –
Caroline Joan – stood on her desk and took up
the speech where Mrs Mackay had left off – *Lend*

me your ears . . . just what the Second Form did
in the opposite room, reciting the Poets Laureate
for Miss Nadimbaba – *John Dryden, Thomas Shadwell,
Nahum Tate, Nicholas Rowe, Laurence Eusden, Colley Cibber,
William Whitehead . . .* but scattering titters and giggles
like noisy confetti on reaching Henry Pye as Caroline Joan
belted out Antony's speech in an Elvis style –
For Brutus, uh huh huh, is an honourable man.
Miss Nadimbaba, no fan of rock 'n' roll, could scarcely
believe her ears, deducing at once that Mrs Mackay
was not with her class. She popped an anxious head
outside her door. Anarchy roared in her face
like a tropical wind. The corridor clock was at four.

The last bell rang. Although they would later regret it,
the teachers, taking their cue from wits-end Mrs Mackay,
allowed the chuckling, bright-eyed, mirthful girls

to go home, reprimand-free, each woman privately glad
that the dark afternoon was over and done,
the chalky words rubbed away to dance as dust
on the air, the dates, the battles, the kings and queens,
the rivers and tributaries, poets, painters, playwrights,
politicos, popes . . . but they all agreed to make it quite clear
in tomorrow's Assembly that foolish behaviour –
even if only the once – wasn't admired or desired
at Stafford Girls' High. Above the school, the moon
was pinned like a monitor's badge to the sky.

Miss Dunn was the first to depart, wheeling
her bicycle through the gates, noticing how
the sky had cleared, a tidy diagram of the Plough
directly above. She liked it this cold, her breath
chiffoning out behind as she freewheeled home
down the hill, her mind emptying itself of geography,
of mountains and seas and deserts and forests
and capital cities. Her small terraced house looked,
she thought, like a sleeping face. She roused it
each evening, kisses of light on its cheeks
from her lamps, the small talk of cutlery, pots
and pans as she cooked, sweet silver steam caressing
the shy rooms of her home. Miss Dunn lived alone.

So did Miss Batt, in a flat on the edge of the park
near the school; though this evening Miss Fife
was coming for supper. The two were good friends
and Miss Fife liked to play on Miss Batt's small piano
after the meal and the slowly shared carafe of wine.
Music and Maths! Johann Sebastian Bach! Miss Batt,
an all-rounder, took out her marking – essays on Henry VIII
and his wives from the Fifth – while Miss Fife gave herself up
to Minuet in G. In between Catherine Howard

and Catherine Parr, Miss Batt glanced across at Fifi's
straight back as she played, each teacher conscious
of each woman's silently virtuous love. Nights like this,
twice a week, after school, for them both, seemed enough.

Mrs Mackay often gave Miss Nadimbaba a lift,
as they both, by coincidence, lived on Mulberry Drive –
Mrs Mackay with her husband of twenty-five grinding,
childless years; Miss Nadimbaba sharing a house
with her elderly aunt. Neither had ever invited
the other one in, although each would politely enquire
after her colleague's invisible half. Mrs Mackay
watched Miss Nadimbaba open her purple door and saw
a cat rubbing itself on her calf. She pulled away
from the kerb, worrying whether Mr Mackay would insist
on fish for his meal. Then he would do his crossword:
Mr Mackay calling out clues – *Kind of court for a bounder (8)* –
while she passed him *Roget, Brewer, Pears*, the *OED*.

The women teachers of England slept in their beds,
their shrewd or wise or sensible heads safe vessels
for Othello's jealousy, the Wife of Bath's warm laugh,
the phases of the moon, the country code;
for Roman numerals, Greek alphabets, French verbs;
for foreign currencies and Latin roots, for logarithms, tables,
quotes; the meanings of *currente calamo* and *fiat lux* and *stet*.
Miss Dunn dreamed of a freezing white terrain
where slowly moving elephants were made of ice.
Miss Nadimbaba dreamed she knelt to kiss Miss Barrett
on her couch and she, Miss Nadimbaba, was Browning
saying *Beloved, be my wife* . . . and then a dog began to bark
and she woke up. Miss Batt dreamed of Miss Fife.

*   *   *

Morning assembly – the world like Quink outside,
the teachers perched in a solemn row on the stage,
the Fifth and Sixth Forms clever and tall, Miss Fife
at the school piano, the Head herself, Doctor Bream,
at the stand – was a serious affair. *Jerusalem* hung
in the air till the last of Miss Fife's big chords
wobbled away. *Yesterday*, intoned Doctor Bream,
*the Lower School behaved in a foolish way, sniggering
for most of the late afternoon.* She glared at the girls
through her pince-nez and paused for dramatic effect.
But the First and Second and Third and Fourth Forms
started to laugh, each girl trying to swallow it down
till the sound was like distant thunder, the opening chord

of a storm. Miss Dunn and Miss Batt, Miss Nadimbaba
and Mrs Mackay leapt to their feet as one, grim-faced.
The Fifth Form hooted and howled. Miss Fife, oddly disturbed,
crashed down fistfuls of furious notes on the yellowing keys.
The Sixth Forms, upper and lower, shrieked. Señora Devizes,
sartorial, strict, slim, severe, teacher of Spanish,
stalked from the stage and stilettoed sharply down
to the back of the Hall to chastise the Fifth and Sixth.
¡Callaos! ¡Callaos! ¡Callaos! ¡Quédense! The whole school
guffawed; their pink young lungs flowering more
than they had for the hymn. *¡El clamor!* The Hall was a zoo.
Snow began falling outside as though the clouds
were being slowly torn up like a rule book. *A good laugh,*

as the poet Ursula Fleur, who attended the school,
was to famously write, *is feasting on air.* The air that day
was chomped, chewed, bitten in two, pulled apart
like a wishbone, licked like a lollipop, sluiced and sucked.
Some of the girls were almost sick. Girls gulped or sipped
or slurped as they savoured the joke. What joke?

Nobody knew. A silly joy sparkled and fizzed. Tabitha Rose,
flower monitor for the day, wet herself, wailed, wept, ran
from the Hall, a small human shower of rain. The bell
for the start of lessons rang. Somehow the school
filed out in a raggedy line. The Head Girl, Josephine June,
scarlet-faced from killing herself, was in for a terrible time
with the Head. Snow iced the school like a giant cake.

No one on record recalls the words that were said,
but Josephine June was stripped of the Head Girl's badge
and sash and sent to the Sixth Form Common Room
to demand of the prefects how they could hope to grow to be
the finest of England's daughters and mothers and wives
after this morning's Assembly's abysmal affair?
But the crowd of girls gave a massive cheer, stamping
the floor with their feet in a rebel beat and Diana Kim,
Captain of Sports, jumped on a chair and declared
that if J.J. was no longer Head Girl then no one
would take her place. *All for one!* someone yelled. *And one
for all!* Diana Kim opened the window and jumped down
into the snow. With a shriek, Emmeline Belle jumped after her,

followed by cackling Anthea Meg, Melanie Hope, Andrea Lyn,
J.J. herself . . . It was Gillian Tess in the Fifth, being lectured
by tight-lipped Señora Devizes on how to behave, who glanced
from the first-floor window and noticed the Sixth Form
bouncing around in the snow like girls on the moon.
A snowball, the size of a netball, was creaking, rolling,
growing under their hands. *Look!* Girls at their windows gaped.
It grew from a ball to the size of a classroom globe. It grew
from a globe to the size of a huge balloon. Miss Dunn,
drumming the world's highest mountains into the heads
of the First Years – *Everest, K2, Kangchenjunga, Lhoste, Makalu 1 . . .*

flung open her window and breathed in the passionate cold
of the snow. A wild thought seeded itself in her head.

In later years, the size of the snowball rolled by the Sixth
grew like a legend. Some claimed that the Head, as it groaned
past her study, thought that there might have been an eclipse.
Ursula Fleur, in her prose poem *Snow,* wrote that it took
the rest of the Michaelmas Term to melt. Miss Batt,
vacantly staring down as her class wrote out a list
of the monarchs of England – *Egbert, Ethelwulf, Ethelbald,*
Ethelbert, Ethelred, Alfred, Edward, Athelstan, Edmund,
Eadred, Eadwig, Edgar . . . noticed the snowball, huge and alone
on the hockey pitch, startlingly white in the pencilly grey
of the light, and thought of desire, of piano scales slowing,
slowing, breasts. She moaned aloud, forgetful of where
she was. Francesca Eve echoed the moan. The class roared.

But that night Miss Batt, while she cooked for Miss Fife,
who was opening the wine with a corkscrew
from last year's school trip to Sienna and Florence,
felt herself naked, electric under her tartan skirt, twin set
and pearls; and later, Miss Fife at the piano, stroking
the first notes of Beethoven's 'Moonlight' Sonata, Miss Batt
came behind her, placing her inked and trembling hands
on her shoulders. A broken A minor chord stumbled
and died. Miss Fife said that Ludwig could only
have written this piece when he was in love. Miss Batt
pulled Miss Fife by the hair, turning her face around, hearing
her gasp, bending down, kissing her, kissing her, kissing her.
Essays on Cardinal Wolsey lay unmarked on the floor.

Across the hushed white park, down the slush of the hill,
Miss Dunn crouched on the floor of her sitting room
over a map of Tibet. The whisky glass in her nervous hand

clunked on her teeth, Talisker sheathing her tongue
in a heroine's warmth. She moved her finger slowly
over the map, the roof of the world. Her fingers walked to Nepal,
changing the mountain *Chomolungma* to *Sagarmatha*.
She sipped at her malt and thought about Mallory, lost
on Everest's slopes with his English Air, of how he'd wanted
to reach the summit *because it was there*. She wondered
whether he had. Nobody knew. She saw herself walking
the upper slopes with the Captain of Sports towards
the foetal shape of a sleeping man . . . She turned to the girl.

*   *   *

That Monday morning Doctor Bream, at her desk,
didn't yet know that the laughter of Stafford Girls' High
would not go away. But when she stood on the stage,
garbed in her Cambridge cap and gown, and told the school
to quietly stand and contemplate a fresh and serious start
to the week, and closed her eyes – the hush like an air balloon
tethered with ropes – a low and vulgar giggle yanked
at the silence. Doctor Bream kept her eyes clenched, hoping
that if she ignored it all would be well. Clumps of laughter
sprouted among the row upon row of girls. Doctor Bream,
determined and blind, started the morning's hymn. *I vow
to thee my country* . . . A flushed Miss Fife started to play.
All earthly things above . . . The rest of the staff joined in –

*entire and whole and perfect, the service of my love,
the love that asks no questions, the love that stands the test* . . .
But the girls were hysterical, watching the Head,
Queen Canute, singing against the tide of their mirth,
their shoals, their glittering laughter. She opened her eyes –
Clarice Maud Bream, MBE, DLitt – and saw, in the giggling sea
one face which seemed to her to be worse, cheekier,

redder and louder, than all of the rest. Nigella Dawn
was fished by the Head from her seat and made to stand
on a chair on the stage. Laughter drained from the Hall. *This girl,*
boomed the Head, *will stand on this chair for as long as it takes
for the school to come to its senses. SILENCE!* The whole school
stood like a crowd waiting for news. The bell rang. Nobody

moved. Nobody made a sound. Minutes slinked away
as Nigella Dawn swayed on her creaky chair. The First Years
stared in shame at their shoes. The Head's tight smile
was a tick. *That,* she thought, in a phrase of her mother's,
has put the tin lid on that. A thin high whine, a kitten,
wind on a wire, came from behind. The school
seemed to hold its breath. Nigella Dawn shook on her chair.
The sound came again, louder. Doctor Bream looked to the staff.
Miss Batt had her head in her lap and was keening and rocking
backwards and forwards. The noise put the Head in mind
of a radio dial – *Luxembourg, Light, Hilversum, Welsh* –
as though the woman were trying to tune in to herself. Miss Batt
flung her head back and laughed, laughed like a bride.

*   *   *

Mr and Mrs Mackay silently ate. She eyed him
boning his fish, slicing it down to the backbone,
sliding the skeleton out, fastidious, deft. She spied him
eat from the right of his plate to the left, ordered, precise.
She clenched herself for his voice. *A very nice dish
from the bottomless deep.* Bad words ran in her head like mice.
She wanted to write them down in the crossword lights.
14 Across: *F . . .* 17 Down: *F . . . . . .* 2 Down: *F . . . . . .*
Mr Mackay reached for the *OED.* She bit her lip. *A word
for one who is given to walking by night, not necessarily
in sleep.* She felt her heart flare in its dark cave, hungry, blind,

open its small beak. *Beginning with* N. Mrs Mackay
moved to the window and stared at the ravenous night. Later,

awake in the beached boat of the marital bed, Mrs Mackay
slid from between the sheets. Her spouse whistled and whined.
She dressed in sweater and slacks, in boots, in her old tweed coat,
and slipped from the house with a tut of the front door snib.
Her breath swaggered away like a genie popped from a flask.
She looked for the moon, found it, arched high over the house,
a raised eyebrow of light, and started to walk. The streets
were empty, darkly sparkling under her feet, ribbons that tied
the sleeping town like a gift. A black cat glared from a wall.
Mrs Mackay walked and walked and walked, letting the night
sigh underneath her clothes, perfume her skin; letting it in,
the scented night – stone, starlight, tree-sleep, rat, owl.
A calm rhythm measured itself in her head. *Noctambulist.*

She walked for hours, till dawn's soft tip rubbed, smudged,
erased the dark. Back home, she stripped and washed
and dressed for school, moving about in the kitchen
till Mr Mackay appeared, requesting a four-minute egg
from a satisfied hen. She watched him slice off the top
with the side of his spoon, dip in his toast, savour the soft gold
of the yolk with his neat tongue. She thought of the girls,
how they'd laughed now for weeks. Panic nipped and salted
her eyes. And later that day, walking among the giggling desks
of the Third, she read Cleopatra's lament in a shaking voice
as tears shone on her cheeks: *Hast thou no care of me?*
Shall I abide in this dull world, which in thy absence is
No better than a sty? O! see my women, the crown

o' the earth doth melt. My lord! O! withered is the garland
of the war, the soldier's pole is fall'n; young boys and girls
are level now with men; the odds is gone, and there is nothing

left remarkable beneath the visiting moon. Carolann Clare, trapped
in a breathless, crippling laugh, seriously thought she would die.
Mrs Mackay lay down her book and asked the girls to start
from the top and carry on reading the play round the class.
She closed her eyes and seemed to drift off at her desk.
The voices of girls shared Shakespeare, line by line, the clock
over the blackboard crumbling its minutes into the dusty air.
From the other side of the wall, light breezes of laughter came
and went. Further away, from the music room, the sound
of the orchestra hooted and sneered its way through Grieg.

Miss Batt, in the staffroom, marking The War of Jenkins' Ear
over and over again, put down her pen. Music reminded her
of Miss Fife. She lay her head on the table, dizzy with lust, longed
for the four o'clock bell, for home, for pasta and *vino rosso*,
for Fifi's body on hers in the single bed, for kisses that tasted
of jotters, of wine. She picked up an essay and read:
*England went to war with Spain because a seaman, Robert
Jenkins, claimed that the Spanish thought him a smuggler
and cut off his ear. He showed the ear in the Commons
and public opinion forced the Government to declare war
on October 23, 1739* . . . Miss Batt cursed under her breath,
slashing a read tick with her pen. The music had stopped. Hilarity
squealed and screeched in its place down the corridor.

Miss Nadimbaba was teaching the poems of Yeats
to the Fifth when the girls in the orchestra laughed. She held
in her hands the poem which had made her a scribbler of verse
at twelve or thirteen. 'The Song' – she was sick of the laughter
at Stafford Girls' High – 'of Wandering Aengus.' She stared
at the girls in her class who were starting to shake. An epidemic,
that's what it was. It had gone on all term. It was now the air
that they breathed, teachers and girls: a giggling, sniggering,
gurgling, snickering atmosphere, a laughing gas that seeped

under doors, up corridors, into the gym, the chemistry lab,
the swimming pool, into Latin and Spanish and French and Greek,
into Needlework, History, Art, R.K., P.E., into cross-country runs,
into the silver apples of the moon, the golden apples of the sun.

Miss Dunn stood with her bike outside school after four,
scanning the silly, cackling girls for a face – Diana Kim's.
The Captain of Sports was tall, red-haired. Her green eyes
stared at Miss Dunn and Miss Dunn *knew*. This was a girl
who would scale a vertical wall of ice with her fingertips,
who would pitch a tent on the lip of a precipice, who would know
when the light was good, when the wind was bad, when snow
was powdery or hard. The girl had the stuff of heroines. Diana Kim
walked with the teacher, pushing her bicycle for her, hearing her
outline the journey, the great adventure, the climb to the Mother
of Earth. Something inside her opened and bloomed.
Miss Dunn was her destiny, fame, a strong hand pulling her
higher and higher into the far Tibetan clouds, into the sun.

*   *   *

Doctor Bream was well aware that something had to be done.
Laughter, it seemed, was on the curriculum. The girls
found everything funny, strange; howled or screamed
at the slightest thing. The Headmistress prowled the school,
listening at classroom doors. The new teacher, Mrs Munro,
was reading The Flaying of Marsyas to the Third: *Help!
Why are you stripping me from myself?* The girls were in fits.
Mrs Munro's tight voice struggled on: *It was possible to count
his throbbing organs and the chambers of his lungs.* Shrieks
and squeals stabbed the air. Why? At what? Doctor Bream
snooped on. Miss Batt was teaching the First Form the names
of the nine major planets: *Mercury, Venus, Earth, Mars,
Jupiter, Saturn, Uranus* . . . Pandemonium hooted and whooped.

The grim Head passed down the corridor, hearing the Fifth Form
gargling its way through the Diet of Worms. She came
to the Honours Board, the names of the old girls written in gold –
Head Girls who had passed into legend, Captains of Sport
who had played the game, prize-winning girls, girls who'd gone on
to achieve great things. Members of Parliament! Blasts of laughter
belched from the playing fields. Doctor Bream walked to her room
and stood by her desk. Her certificates preened behind glass
in the wintery light. Silver medals and trophies and cups gleamed
in the cabinet. She went to the wall – the school photograph
glinted and glowed, each face like a fingertip; the pupils
straight-backed, straight-faced; the staff upright, straight-laced.
A warm giggle burbled outside. She flung open the door.

The empty corridor winked. She could hear
a distant piano practising Für Elise . . . Señora Devizes
counting in Spanish in one of the rooms – *uno, dos, tres,*
cuatro, cinco, seis, siete, ocho, nueve, diez, once, doce,
trece, catorce, quince, diez y seis, diez y siete, diez y ocho . . .
a shrill whistle blowing outside . . . But then a burst of hysteria
came from the classroom above, rolled down the stairs,
exploded again in the classroom below. Mrs Mackay,
frantic, hoarse, could be heard pitching Portia's speech
over the hoots of the Fourth: *The quality of MERCY*
is not STRAINED. It droppeth as the gentle rain from HEAVEN
upon the place BENEATH . . . Cackles, like gunfire, crackled
and spat through the school. A cheer boomed from the Gym.

It went on thus – through every hymn or poem, catechism,
logarithm, sum, exam; in every classroom, drama room
to music room; on school trips to a factory or farm; from
First to Sixth Form, dunce to academic crème de la crème,
day in, day out; till, towards the end of the Hilary Term,

Doctor Bream called yet another meeting in the Staffroom,
determined now to solve the problem of the laughter
of the girls once and for all. The staff filed in at 4.15 –
Miss Batt, Miss Fife, Miss Dunn, Mrs Munro, the sporty
Mrs Lee, Mrs Mackay, Miss Nadimbaba, the Heads of French
and Science – Miss Feaver, Mrs Kaye – Señora Devizes,
the tuneful Miss Aherne, the part-time drama teacher
Mrs Prendergast. The Head stood up and clapped her hands.

Miss Fife poured Earl Grey tea. Miss Dunn stood by the window,
staring out. Miss Batt burned at Miss Fife. Mrs Mackay
sat down and closed her eyes. Miss Nadimbaba churned
the closing couplet of a poem in her head. Miss Feaver
crossed her legs and smiled at Mrs Lee, who twirled
a squash racquet between her rosy knees. *I think we all agree,*
said Doctor Bream, *that things are past the pale. The girls
are learning nothing. Discipline's completely gone
to pot. I'd like to hear from each of you in turn. Mrs Mackay?*
Mrs Mackay opened her eyes and sighed. And shook her head.
And then she started singing: *It was a lover and his lass,
with a hey, and a ho, and a hey nonino, that o'er
the green cornfield did pass, in the spring time,*

*the only pretty ring time, when birds do sing, hey ding
a ding, ding; sweet lovers love the spring.* A silence fell.
Miss Batt looked at Miss Fife and cleared her throat. *Miss Fife
and I are leaving at the end of term.* Miss Dunn at the window
turned. *I'm leaving then myself. To have a crack at Everest . . .*
The Head sank to a chair. Miss Nadimbaba stood. Then one by one
the staff resigned – to publish poetry, to live in Spain, to form
a tennis club, to run a restaurant in Nice, to tread the boards,
to sing in smoky clubs, to translate Ovid into current speech,
to study homeopathy. Doctor Bream was white with shock.

And what, she forced herself at last to say, *about the girls?*
Miss Batt, slowly undressing Fifi in the stockroom in her head,
winked at Miss Fife. She giggled girlishly. Miss Feaver laughed.

*   *   *

Small hours. The moon tracked Mrs Mackay as she reached the edge
of the sleeping town, houses dwindling to fields, the road
twisting up and away into the distant hills. She caught her mind
making anagrams – *grow heed, stab, rats* – and forced herself
to chant aloud as she walked. Hedgerow. Bats. Star. Her head
cleared. The town was below her now, dark and hunched,
a giant husband bunched in his sleep. Mrs Mackay climbed on,
higher and higher, keeping close to the ditch, till the road snaked
in a long *S* then levelled out into open countryside. *Shore,
love, steer, low, master, night loom, riven use, no.* Horse. Vole.
Trees. Owl. Stream. Moonlight. Universe. On. *Wed, loop, wand,
drib, tiles, pay thaw, god.* Dew. Pool. Dawn. Bird. Stile. Pathway.
Dog. She arrived at the fringe of a village as morning broke.

Miss Batt held Miss Fife in her arms at dawn, the small room
chaste with new light. Miss Fife began to talk in her sleep –
*The square on the hypotenuse is equal to the sum
of the squares of the other two sides.* Miss Batt slid down,
nuzzled her breastbone, her stomach, kissed down,
kissed down, down to the triangle. The tutting bedside clock
counted to five. They woke again at seven, stupid with love,
everything they knew – the brightest stars, Sirius, Canopus,
Alpha Centauri, Vega; the Roman Emperors, Claudius,
Nero, Galba, Otho, Vitellius; musical terms, *allegro, calando,
crescendo, glissando*; mathematics, the value of pi,
prime numbers, Cantor's infinities – only a jumble of words,
a jumble of words. A long deep zero groaned from Miss Fife.

Miss Dunn took out her list and checked it again. Her class
was sniggering its way through a test on Britain's largest lakes.
She mouthed her list like a prayer: socks, mittens, shirt, leggings,
hat, face mask, goggles, harness, karabiners, ice screws, pitons,
helmet, descender, ascender, loops, slings, ice axe, gaiters,
crampons, boots, jacket, hood, trousers, water bottle, urine
bottle, waste bags, sleeping bag, kit bag, head torch, batteries,
tent, medical kit, maps, stove, butane, radio, fixing line, rope,
cord, stoppers, wands, stakes and chocks and all of it twice.
A sprinkle of giggles made her look up. *Pass your test to the girl
on your left to be marked. The answers are: Lough Neagh,
Lower Lough Erne, Loch Lomond, Loch Ness, Loch Awe, Upper
Lough Erne* . . . Diana Kim climbed and climbed in her head.

Doctor Bream read through the letter to parents then signed
her name at the end. The school was to close at the end of term
until further notice. A dozen resignation notes from the staff
lay on her desk. The Head put her head in her hands and wept.
A local journalist lurked at the gates. Señora Devizes
and Miss Nadimbaba entered the room to say that the girls
were filing into the Hall for the Special Assembly. There was still
no sign of Mrs Mackay. She looked at the shattered Head
and Kipling sprang to Miss Nadimbaba's lips: *If you can force
your heart and nerve and sinew to serve your turn long after they
are gone* . . . Señora Devizes joined in: *Persiste aun no tengas
fuerza, y sólo te quede la voluntad que les dice:
¡Persiste!* The Head got to her feet and straightened her back.

And so, Doctor Bream summed up, *you girls have laughed this once
great school into the ground. Señora Devizes plans to return
to Spain.* Cries of *¡Olé! Miss Batt and Miss Fife have resigned.*
Wolf whistles. *Mrs Prendergast is joining the Theatre Royale.*
A round of applause crashed on the boards like surf. The Head stared
at the laughing girls then turned and marched from the stage,

clipped up the polished corridor, banged through the double doors,
crunched down the gravel drive to the Staff Car Park and into her car.
Elvis, shrieked Caroline Joan from the Hall, *has left the building*.
A cheer like an avalanche bounced off the roof. The Captain of Sports
slipped from her seat and followed Miss Dunn. The girls burst
into song as their mute teachers walked from the stage. *Till we
have built Jerusalem in England's green and pleasant land.*

*   *   *

The empty school creaked and sighed, its desks the small coffins
of lessons, its blackboards the tombstones of learning. The books
in the Library stiffened and yellowed and curled. The portraits
of gone Headmistresses stared into space. The school groaned,
the tiles on its roof falling off in its sleep, its windows as white
as chalk. The grass on the playing fields grew like grass
on a grave. Doctor Bream stared from her hospital window
over the fields. She could see the school bell in its tower glint
in the evening sun like a tear in an eye. She turned away. Postcards
and get-well messages from the staff were pinned to the wall.
She took down a picture of Everest from Miss Dunn: *We leave
Camp II tomorrow if the weather holds to climb the Corridor
to 21,000 feet. Both coping well with altitude. The Sherpas . . .*

Mrs Mackay walked through Glen Strathfarrar, mad, muttering,
free; a filthy old pack on her back filled with scavenged loot –
banana, bottle, blanket, balaclava, bread, blade, bible. She sat
by a stream, filled her bottle and drank. She ate the crusts,
the fruit. Kingfisher. Eagle. Heron. Red deer. Midge. The Glen
darkened and cooled like History. Mrs Mackay lay in the heather
under her blanket, mumbling lines from Lear: *As mad as the vex'd
sea; singing aloud; crowned with rank fumitor and furrow weeds,
with burdocks, hemlocks, nettles, cuckoo-flowers, darnel . . .*
Syllables. Syllables. Sleep came suddenly, under the huge black,

the chuckling clever stars. The Head at her window looked north
to the clear night sky, to Pollux and Castor, Capella, Polaris,
and wondered again what could have become of Mrs Mackay.

Rough lads from the town came up to the school to throw stones
through the glass. Miss Batt and Miss Fife had moved
to a city. They drank in a dark bar where women danced, cheek
to cheek. Miss Batt loved Miss Fife till she sobbed and shook
in her arms. Stray cats prowled through the classrooms, lunging
at mice. Miss Fife dreamed that the school was a huge ship
floating away from land, all hands lost, steered by a ghost,
a woman whose face was the Head's, was Miss Nadimbaba's,
then Mrs Mackay's, Mrs Lee's, Miss Feaver's, Miss Dunn's,
Mrs Munro's, Mrs Kaye's, Miss Aherne's, Señora Devizes' . . .
She woke in the darkness, a face over hers, a warm mouth
kissing the gibberish from her lips. The school sank in her mind,
a black wave taking it down as she gazed at the woman's face.

Miss Nadimbaba put down her pen and read through her poem.
The palms of her hands felt light, that talented ache. She altered
a verb and the line jumped on the page like a hooked fish. She needed
to type it up, but the poem was done. She was dying
to read it aloud to her aunt. She would open some wine.
In the hospital, a nurse brought warm milk and a pill to the Head,
who stared through the bars at the blackened hulk of the school.
By dawn, at John O'Groats, Mrs Mackay had finally run out of land.
She wrote her maiden name with a stick in the sand then walked
into the sea, steady at first, step by step, till the firm waves lifted her
under her arms and danced her away like a groom with a bride.
High above in the cold sky the seagulls, like schoolgirls, laughed.
Higher again, a teacher fell through the clouds with a girl in her arms.

A Dreaming Week

Not tonight, I'm dreaming
in the heart of the honeyed dark
in a boat of a bed in the attic room
in a house on the edge of the park
where the wind in the big old trees
creaks like an ark.

Not tomorrow, I'm dreaming
till dusk turns into dawn – *dust, must,*
most, moot, moon, mown, down –
with my hand on an open unread book,
a bird that's never flown . . . distantly
the birdsong of the telephone.

Not the following evening, I'm dreaming
in the monocle of the moon,
a sleeping *S* on the page of a bed
in the tome of a dim room, the rain
on the roof, rhyming there,
like the typed words of a poem.

Not the night after that, I'm dreaming
till the stars are blue in the face
printing the news of their old light
with the ink of space,
yards and yards of black silk night
to cover my sleeping face.

Not the next evening, I'm dreaming
in the crook of midnight's arm
like a lover held by another
safe from harm, like a child
stilled by a mother, soft and warm,
twelve golden faraway bells for a charm.

Not that night either, I'm dreaming
till the tides have come and gone
sighing over the frowning sand,
the whale's lonely song
scored on wave after wave of water
all the wet night long.

Not the last evening, I'm dreaming
under the stuttering clock,
under the covers, under closed eyes,
all colours fading to black,
the last of daylight hurrying
for a date with the glamorous dark.

White Writing

No vows written to wed you,
I write them white,
my lips on yours,
light in the soft hours of our married years.

No prayers written to bless you,
I write them white,
your soul a flame,
bright in the window of your maiden name.

No laws written to guard you,
I write them white,
your hand in mine,
palm against palm, lifeline, heartline.

No rules written to guide you,
I write them white,
words on the wind,
traced with a stick where we walk on the sand.

No news written to tell you,
I write it white,
foam on a wave
as we lift up our skirts in the sea, wade,

see last gold sun behind clouds,
inked water in moonlight.
No poems written to praise you,
I write them white.

Gambler

She goes for the sound of the words, the beauty they hold
in the movement they make on the air, the shape
of the breath of a word leaving her lips like a whistle

or kiss. So Hyperion's tips mean nothing to her, the form,
the favourites, whether the going is heavy or firm,
the horse a stinker or first-time blinkered. It's words

she picks, names she ticks. That day it was *Level Headed*
at 10-1, two syllables each to balance the musical chime
of *lev* and *head*, the echoing *el*. She backed it to win

and then on a whim went for *Indian Nectar* at 7-2
to come in next. *Indiannectar. Indiannectar.* She stood
in a trance at the counter, singing it over and over

again in her head which was why, she guessed, she decided
to pick *Sharp Spice* (5-2 fav) to gallop in third – the words
seemed to fit. Most days she sits with her stump of a pen

writing the poems of bets. And how can she lose? Just listen
to some of the names that she didn't choose – *Heiress of Meath,
Springfieldsupreme, Mavis, Shush, Birth of the Blues.*

The Light Gatherer

When you were small, your cupped palms
each held a candlesworth under the skin,
enough light to begin,

                  and as you grew
light gathered in you, two clear raindrops
in your eyes,

            warm pearls, shy,
in the lobes of your ears, even always
the light of a smile after your tears.

Your kissed feet glowed in my one hand,
or I'd enter a room to see the corner you played in
lit like a stage set,

                the crown of your bowed head spotlit.
When language came, it glittered like a river,
silver, clever with fish,

              and you slept
with the whole moon held in your arms for a night light
where I knelt watching.

                Light gatherer. You fell from a star
into my lap, the soft lamp at the bedside
mirrored in you,

and now you shine like a snowgirl,
a buttercup under a chin, the wide blue yonder
you squeal at and fly in,

like a jewelled cave,
turquoise and diamond and gold, opening out
at the end of a tunnel of years.

The Cord

(for Ella)

They cut the cord she was born with
and buried it under a tree
in the heart of the Great Forest
when she was exactly the length
of her mother's nursing elbow
to the tip of her thumb.

She learned to speak and asked them,
though she was young yet,
what the cord had looked like –
had a princess spun it
from a golden spinning wheel?
Could the cord be silver? Was it real?

Real enough and hidden
in the roots of an ancient oak,
the tangled knot of a riddle
or the weird ribbon of a gift
in a poke. As she grew, she asked again
if the cord was made of rope,

then stared from the house she lived in
across the fields to the woods
where rooks spread their pages of wings
like black unreadable books
and the wind in the grass
scribbled sentences wherever she looked.

So she went on foot to the forest
and pressed her ear to the ground,
but not a sound or a movement,
not a breath or a word
gave her a hint where she should go
to hunt for her cord. She went deeper

into the forest, following a bird
which disappeared, a waving hand; shadows
blurred into one huge darkness,
but the stars were her mother's eyes
and the screech of an owl in the tree above
was the sound of a baby's cry.

Wish

But what if, in the clammy soil, her limbs
grew warmer, shifted, stirred, kicked off
the covering of earth, the drowsing corms,
the sly worms, what if her arms reached out
to grab the stone, the grooves of her dates
under her thumb, and pulled her up? I wish.
Her bare feet walk along the gravel path
between the graves, her shroud like washing
blown onto the grass, the petals of her wreath
kissed for a bride. Nobody died. Nobody
wept. Nobody slept who couldn't be woken
by the light. If I can only push open this heavy door
she'll be standing there in the sun, dirty, tired,
wondering why do I shout, why do I run.

North-West

However it is we return to the water's edge
where the ferry grieves down by the Pier Head,
we do what we always did and get on board.
The city drifts out of reach. A huge silvery bird,
a kiss on the lip of the wind, follows our ship.
This is where we were young, the place no map
or heritage guide can reveal. Only an X on a wave
marks the spot, the flowers of litter, a grave
for our ruined loves, unborn children, ghosts.
We look back at the skyline wondering what we lost
in the hidden streets, in the rented rooms,
no more than punters now in a tourist boom.
Above our heads the gulls cry *yeah yeah yeah*.
Frets of light on the river. Tearful air.

Death and the Moon

(for Catherine Marcangeli)

The moon is nearer than where death took you
at the end of the old year. Cold as cash
in the sky's dark pocket, its hard old face
is gold as a mask tonight. I break the ice
over the fish in my frozen pond, look up
as the ghosts of my wordless breath reach
for the stars. If I stood on the tip of my toes
and stretched, I could touch the edge of the moon.

I stooped at the lip of your open grave
to gather a fistful of earth, hard rain,
tough confetti, and tossed it down. It stuttered
like morse on the wood over your eyes, your tongue,
your soundless ears. Then as I slept my living sleep
the ground gulped you, swallowed you whole,
and though I was there when you died,
in the red cave of your widow's unbearable cry,

and measured the space between last words
and silence, I cannot say where you are. Unreachable
by prayer, even if poems are prayers. Unseeable
in the air, even if souls are stars. I turn
to the house, its windows tender with light, the moon,
surely, only as far again as the roof. The goldfish
are tongues in the water's mouth. The black night
is huge, mute, and you are further forever than that.